A Healing Stream Will Flow

Reflections & Songs
For The Hurting Heart

Mark Solfelt, MD

A Healing Stream Will Flow
© Mark Solfelt, MD
First Edition, 2023

All rights reserved. No portion of this book may be reproduced, stored in a retrieval system, or transmitted in any form or by any means—electronic, mechanical, photocopy, recording, scanning, or other—except for brief quotations in critical reviews or articles, without the prior written permission of the publisher.

Published in the United States by Mark Solfelt, MD.

Scripture quotations are taken from the Holy Bible, New Living Translation, copyright ©1996, 2004, 2015 by Tyndale House Foundation. Used by permission of Tyndale House Publishers, Carol Stream, Illinois 60188. All rights reserved.

Hand-lettered artwork: Lauren Ibach

Printed in Minneapolis, MN

ISBN: 979-8-218-24258-9

Contents

Introduction 5

Chapter 1: The Healing Touch of God 8

Chapter 2: The Big Question & The Big Answer 16

Chapter 3: A Suffering Skeptic Believes 21

Chapter 4: When There Are No Words 28

Chapter 5: God Understands 33

Chapter 6: It Was Never Meant to End This Way 40

Chapter 7: Angola 47

Chapter 8: Grace 54

Chapter 9: Invitation 63

Chapter 10: A Healing Stream Will Flow 68

Chapter 11: Receiving the Gift of Life 76

Epilogue: The Anchor 83

About the Author 90

As you read this book, please visit our website at
www.healingstreamevent.com
to listen to the songs and to obtain concert information.

Introduction

Stories and poems? I'm suffering through one of the most difficult times of my life, and you're giving me stories and poems? Like that will take away my sickness and pain, or bring back the loved one I've lost, or end my loneliness, or help me get out of debt? I hardly have time to read or reflect when times are good! And poetry in the midst of chaos and suffering? What good can it do?

Let me briefly explain the origin and nature of this little book you hold in your hands.

I have worked as a heart and lung surgeon for 30 years. I chose the specialty because I wanted to serve people in their times of deepest need. I've cared for people facing crisis and change, some with a good prognosis for recovery, and some who are staring into their own mortality. I have cried with families over a sudden death and walked with patients through years of chronic illness. I have sat with countless patients knowing that the biopsy results I had to share would change their lives forever. I have ministered to patients from all walks of life and all different ethnicities,

Introduction

religions, and world views. Serving two inner-city hospitals, I have cared for rich and poor. I've seen life change in a moment for a teenager who was just out for a joy ride, and I've seen disease come along to break up the party of 65-year marriages. It has been the richest privilege and the highest calling I could ever have imagined, although at times it has pushed me to the edge of my own strength. It has deepened my love for people, and it has definitely strengthened my hope in God.

In addition to my life in medicine, I have been a musician since childhood. I started writing music in middle school, and have been performing original piano and vocal music my entire adult life. When I write a song, it is a curious experience. My songs almost always come to me as a complete package of melody and lyric over the course of half an hour. Boom! I get an idea, rush to the piano, and within minutes the song is born. I may spend the next several weeks smoothing out the edges and refining the poetry, but the creative process for me is generally sudden and unpredictable. And so it flows directly from my life, and reflects my passions and beliefs. Since I live, eat, and breathe in the realm of human suffering, my songs are almost always about finding God in the middle of that journey.

I've noticed a curious thing through my years in medicine. No matter how non-religious people may be in their daily lives, they are more open to the spiritual when faced with the crisis of suffering. Even atheistic patients often appreciate and accept offers of prayer. We live in a culture that is generally becoming more and more terrified of suffering and sees no value in it. We are focused on "quality of life," usually defined as the ideal active life we envision when we're in tip-top shape. But when you speak to people who are re-engaging with loved ones and

Introduction

rediscovering faith in trying times, they will often tell you they are actually grateful for their suffering, because it has opened their eyes to wonders of love and spiritual growth that they could never see before. What a paradox – to hear dying patients say they feel like the most fortunate person in the world! I've heard that many, many times. Clearly there is meaning in suffering if we are open to finding it.

This book you hold was written for your comfort. It was written to answer the question, "Where is God in my suffering?" It was written to bring hope, and to encourage you to consider the possibility that God is reaching out and drawing you into a deeper relationship with Him. The poems are the lyrics to songs I have written, and the stories explain their inspiration. Since the poems are anchored in music and rhythm, try reading them out loud for fullest effect. On page 4 you will find a QR code that provides a link to my website, where you can listen to the songs themselves and find concert information as well. I love the way music touches my senses and opens my emotions. I hope all the facets of this book and the music help bring you closer to God. One thing I want you to know above all else, even if this is the last sentence you choose to read – God sees you in your suffering, and He deeply loves you and desires to minister to you in your darkest hour.

CHAPTER 1

The Healing Touch of God

Jesus was likely in His early 30's when He entered His public ministry. As that time grew near, He underwent an intense period of final preparation that included some incredible highs and some very deep lows. First, He was baptized by John, and saw the Spirit of God descending like a dove. An approving voice came from heaven, "You are my Son, whom I love; with you I am well-pleased." But there was no time to bask in the glow of His Father's love. Immediately the Spirit sent Him into the desert, surrounded by wild animals, to face temptation from Satan for 40 days while fasting. Satan relentlessly maneuvered to gain Jesus' allegiance, tempting Him with tantalizing promises of power, privilege, and pleasure. We cannot know what Jesus faced in that crucible of misery, but the Bible says He was tempted in every way we are, yet without sin. There's a loneliness and suffering in temptation that can be short-circuited simply by giving in to it. Suffering temporarily ends – guilt ensues. But Jesus did not give in to the temptation. He endured the suffering and emerged from the desert guilt-free, ready to reveal the grace and truth of God in human form. And He chose not to enter the task alone. He selected a team of disciples, with the intention that these first-followers would someday establish His church after He had departed. Their status as eyewitnesses to miracle after miracle, their opportunity to hear and record the actual teachings of God on Earth, gave them the credibility and courageous faith they would someday need to lead the church.

Uniquely endorsed by His Father, uniquely engaged in all facets of human temptation and suffering, and uniquely encouraged by the comradery of His newly assembled team, Jesus launched His public ministry. Not with fanfare or self-promotion, but in humility and obscurity. And not from the pulpit, but at the bedside. Jesus threw Himself at the chaos of sin that is reflected in human illness and suffering. If one wants to fix what sin has broken, one needs to look no further than this. Human illness is the great equalizer, as universal to mankind as the sin that causes it. Suffering does not respect boundaries of culture, location, bank account, or the square footage of one's home. Jesus attacked it head-on: fever, leprosy, paralysis, and various other diseases. Many were miraculously healed in a time when medical practice created more misery than benefit. People were attracted to Jesus in their desperation and need, and as they lingered in His healing presence they were amazed at the clarity and authority of His teaching.

By ministering to those who were suffering and surrounding Himself with outcasts, Jesus stood out against a culture in which sick people were ostracized, separated from community, and often assumed to be sinful or morally defective human beings. And as for the prostitutes, corrupt tax collectors, and other obvious sinners - they were considered beneath contempt. Yet here was Jesus, God in human flesh, immersing Himself in the world of suffering and pain, healing all comers, turning lives around who truly had no legitimate hope. There was no modern medical process – no diagnostic testing or effective treatment regimens for these people. They were destined to suffer until they died, their diseases progressing mercilessly. Not surprisingly, they flocked to Jesus and crowded around Him everywhere He went. The Gospel of Mark 5:24-34 tells a particularly amazing story about Jesus in this setting:

> All the people were following him, crowding around him. A woman in the crowd had suffered for twelve years with constant bleeding. She had suffered a great deal from many doctors, and over the years she had spent everything she had to pay them, but she had gotten no better. In fact, she had gotten worse. She had heard about Jesus, so she came up behind him through the crowd and touched his robe. For she thought to herself, "If I can just touch his robe, I will be healed." Immediately the bleeding stopped, and she could feel in her body that she had been healed of her terrible condition. Jesus realized at once that healing power had gone out from him, so he turned around in the crowd and asked, "Who touched my robe?" His disciples said to him, "Look at this crowd pressing around you. How can you ask, 'Who touched me?'" But he kept on looking around to see who had done it. Then the frightened woman, trembling at the realization of what had happened to her, came and fell to her knees in front of him and told him what she had done. And he said to her, "Daughter, your faith has made you well. Go in peace. Your suffering is over."

As a physician, I immediately speculate as to the source of the woman's bleeding. Whatever it was, it was not severe enough to take her life after 12 years. It was a chronic, slow blood loss which undoubtedly left her profoundly anemic, weak, and tired. She was likely very pale, perhaps thin and frail, old beyond her years. She had been wealthy enough to consult many doctors, but they had bled her dry in a different way with "remedies" that only added to her suffering. I imagine in that moment of healing, Jesus was thorough. He stopped the bleeding completely. He removed the festering underlying cause. He brought her hemoglobin and iron stores up to normal. He corrected her laboratory values and reversed any secondary complications of her illness. And she felt the physical difference immediately.

But was there a deeper healing that occurred? Jesus said her faith had healed her – faith in what? The Bible defines faith as being sure of what we hope for and certain of what we do not see. Her faith was in Jesus. Certainly not in herself, her doctors, or in the power of positive thinking after 12 years. She had seen enough and heard enough of Jesus to be sure that a mere touch of His robe would be sufficient to heal her. Informed by what she had witnessed in the lives of others, she was certain of what she could not see – His power and love. Her sincere hope was this: What Jesus had done for others; He would do for her. And when He did, she was so overwhelmed that she fell at His feet, trembling with the realization of what He had done. "Go in peace," Jesus said. "Your suffering is over."

I believe that each one of us, at some point in our lives, needs to experience the healing touch of God. It's the point where we come to the end of ourselves, when we are facing something bigger than we can handle. When no one seems to have an answer. When our strength is gone, and the strongest thing about us is our fear.

When we recall the experiences of others who have turned to faith and wonder if God would work for us. When we feel the inclination to cry out to God, even when we're not sure He's there. Of course, the healing touch of God goes deeper than the physical realm to the root cause of it all – our sin. The forgiveness and love of God, and the hope of eternal life in Him, allows us to "go in peace" when we fall at His feet trembling with the realization of who He really is. This is the healing that matters most.

The bleeding woman was healed of her specific illness, but likely fell ill again as her age advanced. She passed away as we all do. But her faith had cured her ultimate fatal disease – the curse of sin – and enabled her to spend eternity in the presence of God Himself. The Bible says it is appointed for us to die once, and that physical death is inevitable, as we all know. We still seek healing and fight to retain every ability we can for as long as it is possible. This is the unquenchable will to live, and live well, that God has placed in every human soul. But it's meant to draw us to something more – to immortality, to eternal life through God's forgiveness. That is how suffering leads to perfect peace, and faith leads to ultimate healing.

Perhaps you are at the same point in your suffering as the woman in the crowd – desperate for a touch of healing and love from the hand of God, and for the hope of eternal life. I encourage you to continue in this little book with the same dogged persistence she had. Press your way through the distractions that are crowding around you – even your own pain. Don't be distracted by those who would ostracize or judge you in your struggle. Suffering of all kinds can be the most isolating experience. Sometimes people run from us in our sufferings because they are afraid to face their own pain, or are afraid to acknowledge the pain all around them. But true followers of Jesus will surround you with love and compassion because they know they were outcasts touched by the love of God and adopted into His family. They humbly and lovingly long for you to experience the same relationship with Him. Try not to let fear of failure and the burdens of the past distract you and cause you to lose hope. The woman in the crowd persevered, even after she had spent everything she had on useless medical treatments over a twelve-year struggle! But her best decision was to put all that behind and reach out to Jesus. She went from a face in the crowd to one He called "daughter." Follow her example and reach out to Him, because He loves you and sees you. He will feel the touch of your hand and meet you in your suffering.

Here Today

If you're here today with a broken heart
If you're here today with suffering and pain
If you're here today because you need a new start
You need a touch of God's Spirit above all
And that is why you came

We're here today to stand by your side
And proclaim the power of courage and love
We're here today to lay down our pride
To open our hearts to the voice of God above

And there's no perfect person in this place
There are tears and fears all around
But if you're looking for somewhere to be loved as you are
You found it here!

We're here today to see who we are
As we gaze into God's beautiful face
We're here to give our all in this hour
Because he gave everything to us here today.

He said to her, "Daughter, your faith has made you well. Go in peace. Your suffering is over."

Mark 5:34

CHAPTER 2
The Big Question & The Big Answer

It's a fair question that often comes to mind when we're suffering: Where is God? If He's loving, how can He watch me struggle? If He's powerful, why doesn't He intervene? Our suffering seems to indicate a deficiency in God, and it undermines our trust in His infinite power and love. Even the Psalmist expressed this confusion:

> "O Lord, why do you stand so far away?
> Why do you hide when I am in trouble?" — Psalm 10:1

If you listen to some of the loudest voices in our society today, they suggest that Christianity has absolutely nothing to say about suffering, so if you have doubts about the relevance of faith at this difficult time in your life you are not alone. But actually the opposite is true! Jesus came expressly because we face suffering, both temporary in this life and eternal in the life to follow. He engaged with our suffering and took it on Himself to provide a way of escape for us. It wasn't with a magic wand that God demonstrated His love and power and delivered us from the curse of death. It was through the suffering, death, and resurrection of His only Son, Jesus. This is the core message of Christian faith. Our own rebellion against God brought illness and death into the world and threatened to drive an eternal wedge between God and man. Christianity is all about God's intervention in human history to literally save us from eternal suffering. It took a tremendous love - a very personal love - for God to give His Son as a sacrifice, and it took great power to raise Him up from the dead.

> "For this is how God loved the world: He gave his one and only Son, so that everyone who believes in him will not perish but have eternal life. God sent his Son into the world not to judge the world, but to save the world through him."
> — John 3:16-17

Jesus is God's answer to our suffering.

I will never forget an experience I had many years ago at a hospital where I did heart surgery. One morning I was emergently called to the ER for a man who had collapsed due to a cardiac arrest. When I arrived at his bedside, the staff were trying furiously to resuscitate him, but after almost an hour with no response, and no opportunity to stabilize him for surgery, he died. It took a while to gather his family from work and home. His children arrived first, and the last to arrive was his elderly wife. I gently led her into the room to see her husband's body and I sat with her while she grieved. It turns out he had just retired. We sat there for quite a long time, and then she shocked me. She looked up at me and said, "Wake him up. It's time to go home. Get him up! I want to take him home. Wake him up!" Her family stepped in at that moment to comfort her. I was struck by our helplessness in the face of illness and death, and all I could think of was the power of God who raised Christ from the dead. As gently as I could, I told her again that her husband was gone, and there was nothing in my power that could reverse that fact. He could not be awakened, and she could not take him home.

I don't have the power to wake a man from the dead. I don't have power over death. I can't stop the cells in a person's body from breaking down and decaying. I can't summon his spirit and put it back into his body. I can't breathe life into a man and re-animate him after he has passed away. No man can do that for another man. But GOD CAN, and He proved it when He raised Jesus His Son from the grave. I sent that poor woman home empty-handed and broken-hearted that day, but it is the hope of all who believe that we will live eternally with Him, and that we will be reunited with loved ones. In other words, those we have lost we will see again! And this hope of eternal life and reconciliation with God and our loved ones - this is one of the great joys of the Christian message! Our God is not deficient in our suffering. He is all-sufficient and powerful, even to the point that He has overcome death itself!

For Our Good

You ask me:

   "How can a God of love turn a blinded eye to my suffering?
   And how can a God of peace watch this storm rage?
   And how can a God of power stand idly by and watch me cry?
   I wonder why you call him 'Lord!'
   Because it seems to me that a God of love
   Would wipe away every bitter tear
   And it seems to me that a God of peace
   Would conquer hate and calm my fear
   And it seems to me that a God of power
   Would finally break the spell and make all things well
   Well, why wouldn't he?"

I'll answer:

   "God so loved the world that He gave his only beloved Son
   So whoever believes in Him will have forever peace.
   And no man can overcome death's power, but Jesus could!
   And all that power, and all that peace, and all that love
   He gave to us for our good."

For this is how God loved the world: He gave his one And Only Son

John 3:16

CHAPTER 3
A Suffering Skeptic Believes

Many people are skeptical of faith because they see suffering as evidence of a deficiency in God. He is either uncaring and imperfect in His love - having the power to change our painful circumstances and choosing not to - or He would like to change our situation but lacks the power to do it. Several years ago, I encountered such a skeptic, and our interaction left a permanent mark on my heart.

Jerry was a man of the world – intelligent, strong-willed, creative, independent. His independence was borne of a painful childhood. His father was an abusive, alcoholic pedophile, and the miseries of his home life caused Jerry to leave at a young age and never look back. He put his faith in his own strength and abilities, and in the power of his mind. He became well-known in his career and devoted everything to that success and recognition. He had a family, but in time he left them behind and immersed himself in work and his own drinking habit. He found himself isolated and alone. Unable to forget or process the sadness of his bitter past, he drowned the memories in alcohol and drug abuse. There was, however, one ray of hope in his life. He had a dedicated sister, Sue, who was a nurse anesthetist. She had emerged from the same heartbreaking childhood and had found the acceptance and love of her Heavenly Father through faith in Jesus Christ. Sue consistently and gently tried to nudge her brother toward the love of God, but he scoffed his disapproval and disbelief. Who could blame him? Where was God in the darkest moments of his past?

Cancer came and changed everything for Jerry. Perhaps due to his drinking, he developed a particularly vicious cancer of the tongue and floor of his mouth. It progressed relentlessly despite all attempts at treatment, making it increasingly difficult to eat or maintain his weight and strength. The tumor became more and more painful and disfiguring. He reached a point where he could no longer work or live independently, and he moved in with Sue. She selflessly cared for him and endured his flashes of anger, which she correctly perceived as expressions of desperation and fear. And as always, she invited him to consider Jesus. It was excruciating for her to watch this proud man suffer and deteriorate without hope. Sue and I worked together in the operating room, but I was unaware of the situation until she approached me about Jerry. It wasn't medical advice she was seeking. She wanted me to talk to Jerry about God.

This was a difficult assignment. I did not know this man. I had no basis upon which to intrude on his suffering, except that I was a friend of his sister. After much prayer, I came up with a plan. I wrote him a letter, acknowledging his skepticism and pain. I explained why I, as a man of science and medicine, had given my life to Jesus. I explained the paradox and mystery of faith – that until one takes a step of faith toward God, it is impossible to truly know Him. With letter in hand, I visited him one day as he lay in his hospital bed. I introduced myself as Sue's friend, expressed my sympathy, told him my family was praying for him, and asked him if he would read a letter, which I left on his bedside table. The visit was short and a bit awkward – he was courteous, but I had a sense he would not read the letter. In fact, he did not read it or mention it to Sue, but he also did not throw it away. He saved it, and six months later when he was close to death, he finally read the letter! He told Sue that he wouldn't mind visiting with me again. He had just endured a crisis in which he almost suffocated from the swelling in his mouth and throat. He was in the hospital, doing poorly, terrified, and fearful of death.

I found Jerry to be much altered when we met again in his hospital room. I could tell his journey was nearing the end, but there was a change in his demeanor. He was ready to take that first step of faith. He was eager to clear the air between himself and his Creator but was convinced that after resisting God's grace for so many years, he was not worthy of forgiveness. He had so many regrets, so many lost opportunities. What a joy it was to share with him the message of Romans 5:8 and Romans 8:38-39:

> But God showed his great love for us by sending Christ to die for us while we were still sinners...I am convinced that nothing can ever separate us from God's love. Neither death nor life, neither angels nor demons, neither our fears for today nor our worries about tomorrow—not even the powers of hell can separate us from God's love. No power in the sky above or in the earth below—indeed, nothing in all creation will ever be able to separate us from the love of God that is revealed in Christ Jesus our Lord.

Gradually as we talked, Jerry began to see things from God's perspective. We all have sinned; we all fall short. We all wander astray into danger, like sheep without a shepherd. God has stepped in to do what we could never do on our own. He paid the full penalty for our rebellion, offering forgiveness instead of condemnation, and communion instead of eternal separation. It was amazing that years of proud denial of the existence of God had done nothing to erase the burden of guilt and regret in Jerry's soul. But even more amazing was the miraculous power of divine grace and mercy that melted his pride and resistance into humility and repentance. It was difficult for him to speak, painful for him to even swallow, but that day he bowed his head and cried out to God in very simple phrases of worship and confession. And when he had finished, he lifted his head with a sigh of utter relief and a face of radiant joy, and simply said, "Ah, to be forgiven!"

What happened that day in Jerry's hospital room was a visible and palpable spiritual transformation like I had never seen. He had found the loving, protecting Father he had never known. Jerry and I started that three-hour visit as distant acquaintances and ended as brothers, both changed by God's amazing love. He died three weeks later, but Sue tells me he was a different man in that time. Jerry was calm, peaceful, humble, ready. From that day in the hospital until he died, he would always assure Sue, "Don't worry, Sue! I know where I'm going!" And he was peaceful in his suffering. He died just before Easter, which he celebrated in Heaven in full view of his wonderful Savior. No longer a skeptic but surrounded by the power of God's redeeming love!

Nothing in all creation will ever be able to separate us from the love of God that is revealed in Christ Jesus our Lord.

Romans 8:39

Can We Talk About Jesus?

He was a strong man with a strong hand
He never needed anyone
He thought if he worked hard, he would go far
He knew how to get things done
He had a family, but in time he chose to leave them all behind
He put his faith in his own strength, and the power of his mind

But he had a sister, and like a sister
She never missed her chance to say
That God loved him, she wouldn't give in
Even when he pushed away
She spoke out in courage, it was the courage of a simple, loving faith
She'd give him time to speak his mind, and then she'd gently say:

Can we talk about Jesus? Can we talk about my best friend?
Can we talk of forgiveness? Can we talk about happy endings?
Can we talk about heaven, even though you're not sure that it's true?
Can we talk about Jesus, and Jesus' love for you?

It happened one morning, without a warning
It seemed like any other day
But something was wrong, and then at the doctor,
He was shocked to hear him say,
"I'm sorry, it's cancer, and there's no answer that will turn it all around."
And suddenly this proud man's world was spinning upside down.

But he had a sister, and like a sister
She came rushing to his side
He was unkind because he was hiding
All the fear he felt inside
But she lovingly served him,
And shared the burden of his anger and his pain
She prayed his mind would open wide, and then she said again:

Can we talk about Jesus? Can we talk about my best friend?
Can we talk of forgiveness? Can we talk about happy endings?
Can we talk about heaven, even though you're not sure that it's true?
Can we talk about Jesus, and Jesus' love for you?

Sometimes a man's story is filled with glory,
And then it turns to sudden fear
And he starts to listen to the wisdom he rejected for years
And he starts to know his darkest moment is a blessing in disguise
It softens up the hardest heart and opens up his eyes

And so, he finally became a seeker,
Though he grew weaker by the hour
He saw his need for a Redeemer,
He could feel the Spirit's power
And he cried, "Savior, in your mercy, come and take my sins away.
It's so good to be forgiven!" is all that he could say.

Now he's walking with Jesus, now he's talking to his best friend
Now he's freely forgiven, now he's living the happy ending
Now he's singing in Heaven, and he knows that God's Word is true
Now he's worshiping Jesus, and what Jesus' love can do!
Now he's worshiping Jesus, and what Jesus' love can do!
Can we talk about Jesus, and Jesus' love for you?

CHAPTER 4

When There Are No Words

Sometimes in the middle of trials and suffering we can't talk about what we're going through. There are no words to express the depth of our fear or the extent of our anguish. Several years ago, on a sunny August day, my wife and I received a call from two of our dearest friends, Mike and Sharon. They called to tell us shocking news. Earlier that afternoon they had lost their wonderful, exuberant 12-year-old son Noah in a tragic accident. They were literally in the last few minutes of a vacation, car packed and ready to head home. Their son took one last ride in a golf cart that flipped over and landed on his chest, crushing him. In that one terrifying and heartbreaking moment their lives changed forever. As my wife and I walked through that grief with our friends, it was immediately obvious that we had no words. No words could ever begin to express what they were feeling. No words could heal their pain. We had no words to pretend that we understood because we knew we couldn't understand. There were no words to express the anguish at such a senseless turn of events - one that turned a time of fun into a nightmare and cut short a life full of promise and joy. Maybe you are in that place right now – suffering an illness or fear or loss that is beyond words, and therefore seems beyond comfort. The Bible says that God understands what you are feeling, because He also experienced unspeakable suffering, pain, and loss. He came and lived among us in a tangible, physical, and broken world. He experienced injustice, oppression, hatred, prejudice, physical torture, and temptation. Jesus understands. This truth is at the heart of one of my favorite Bible verses, Hebrews 4:15-16:

> This High Priest of ours understands our weaknesses, for he faced all the same testings we do, yet he did not sin. So let us come boldly to the throne of our gracious God. There we will receive his mercy, and we will find grace to help us when we need it most.

When we are at a point where we cannot bear our pain or even put it into words, we are invited to confidently approach God, who understands our suffering. He has been tempted in every way that we can be. We do not need eloquent prayers in that moment, because the Holy Spirit prays on our behalf! As it says in Romans 8:26-27:

> And the Holy Spirit helps us in our weakness. For example, we don't know what God wants us to pray for. But the Holy Spirit prays for us with groanings that cannot be expressed in words. And the Father who knows all hearts knows what the Spirit is saying, for the Spirit pleads for us believers in harmony with God's own will.

The significance of these verses cannot be overstated. God knows our hearts, and the Holy Spirit pleads for us with groanings that cannot be expressed in words! Many times in my life I have been too burned out or too confused by circumstances to even know what to pray for. How amazing to picture the Holy Spirit praying on my behalf, even when there are no words to be found! This all-sufficient grace and comfort of God - this peace that passes all understanding – was beautifully evident in the lives of our friends who lost their son Noah on that tragic summer afternoon. In the days surrounding his funeral and the months that followed, although honest in the pain of their grief, Mike and Sharon were a constant encouragement to those who came alongside them. God gave *them* the words! They spoke of the reality of God's presence in their lives. Noah had placed his faith in Jesus for the forgiveness of his sins, and they had incredible joy when they envisioned his current reality in the presence of his Savior in Heaven. They reminded us of the hope of I Corinthians 2:9:

> No eye has seen, no ear has heard, and no mind can imagine what God has prepared for those who love him.

We cannot imagine what God has prepared for those who love Him, because it exceeds anything we have ever seen or heard. No doubt when we experience it someday, it will leave us speechless – no longer with a profound grief, but with an inexpressible joy!

This High Priest of ours understands our weaknesses, for he faced all of the same testings we do, yet he did not sin.

Hebrews 4:15

I Have No Words

I have no words
For a grief so profound, for a wound so deep,
    for a pain so immense
I have no words
For this smothering fear, for a loss so severe,
    for a trial so intense
So I will sit by you quietly, and pray while you cry
I will share in your suffering when you're dying inside

The meaningless hopelessness of it all!
Where is God's answer when we call?
We make every effort, so who is to blame?
Is a life well-lived an unwinnable game?
And where is God in my suffering?
Where is God?

I have no words
For a God who would see His children in need
And give His own life in their place
I have no words
For a love so strong it can right every wrong,
And fill us with healing and grace
And he knows our weakness, He's here when we cry
He took our suffering; He was willing to die

The meaningless hopelessness of it all –
He is the answer to our call!
He made the effort – He took the blame
He bore our burden of unspeakable pain
And there is God in our suffering!

Yes, there is God!

CHAPTER 5

God Understands

I grew up in the 60's and 70's in the City of Edina, which is a suburb of Minneapolis. In those years, Edina was an idyllic community with several enclaves of old-money affluence mixed in with tidy middle-class subdivisions like my neighborhood. It was a town rich in financial resources, but it was also rich in student talent, since the high school was one of the largest in Minnesota. That combination led to uncommon levels of success in athletics, with frequent state championships in almost every sport. Hockey is huge in the Land of 10,000 Lakes (think high school football in Texas), and the annual High School Hockey Tournament is a major state-wide event. Needless to say, there was resentment and jealousy aimed our way when we made the tournament almost every year and won it every 2-3 years. Edina kids were known state-wide as "cake eaters," an insult famously included in the classic hockey movie *The Mighty Ducks*. The term implies arrogant wealth, privilege, and indifference to the plight of those less fortunate, like Marie Antoinette infamously suggesting "let them eat cake" when told the peasants were starving without bread to eat.

I had a lovely childhood in Edina, to be sure. It was not, however, a childhood free of insecurity or pain. My wonderful Dad was a man of great charisma, confidence, and delightful self-effacing humor. He suffered a huge heart attack when I was nine years old, and although he survived, his career and his vigor were never quite the same. He ultimately died of heart failure when I was 27 years old. My Mom was a bright and cheerful woman with a sunny disposition and a very real and practical faith. She taught us to see God in everyday blessings and to seek Him in everyday challenges. Surprisingly, she also struggled with unpredictable bouts of paralyzing major depression. In those days people did not discuss or even admit to mental illness, and there was a definite stigma that prevented us from opening up about it to even our closest friends. In Mom's case, her depression and anxiety stemmed from a traumatic childhood marred by her father's alcoholism and her parent's eventual divorce. Despite all their trials, Mom and Dad approached life with faith and love, humor and joy, and much optimism for the future. We had a happy homelife, even though it was punctuated by some times of very intense uncertainty and suffering.

I certainly did not feel like a "cake-eater." I developed a keen sense of compassion and empathy for those who are suffering, and my family was never indifferent to the struggles of those around us. Appearances are seldom what they seem, and generalizations never explain the messy details of individual life experience. Edina was a great place to grow up, but I'm sure behind every front door in every neighborhood there were secrets and struggles, disappointments, and fears. Amazingly, through frugality and hard work, my Mom and Dad provided everything we needed despite Dad's career being derailed by illness. We were not affluent like many in Edina, but we felt richly blessed. At the center of our family life was the assurance that our loving God saw us, understood our trials, and had unlimited resources to deliver us and to provide whatever we needed.

Many people think of God as a sort of celestial cake-eater - powerful, rich, unaware of our plight, and indifferent to our true needs. Nothing could be farther from the truth. The Bible paints a picture of a loving God who is forgiving and compassionate, understanding, and eager to help. Does this description in Psalm 103:8-14 match your concept of God?

> The Lord is compassionate and merciful,
> slow to get angry and filled with unfailing love.
> He will not constantly accuse us,
> nor remain angry forever.
> He does not punish us for all our sins:
> He does not deal harshly with us, as we deserve.
> For his unfailing love toward those who fear him
> is as great as the height of the heavens above the earth.
> He has removed our sins as far from us
> as the east is from the west.
> The Lord is like a father to his children,
> tender and compassionate to those who fear him.
> For he knows how weak we are;
> he remembers we are only dust.

God sees the bigger picture of our lives. He uses the dark times to draw us to Him, and to refine our faith. In our weakness He is strong, and when we are overwhelmed by fear He comforts with His presence. He has a plan, but in the confusion of difficult circumstances it can be hard to see. When my Dad was in the later stages of heart failure, I was living in Grand Rapids, Michigan and was working long hours as a surgical resident. Every time I had a week off, I would rush to the airport to come home so I could be with him. Because of the effect of Lake Michigan, Grand Rapids is one of the cloudiest places in the country in the winter months, rivaling Seattle with days on end of dense gray skies. By contrast, Minneapolis is often intensely sunny even in the most frigid cold of winter. I would board the plane in that gloomy weather with great anticipation, knowing that within a few minutes of take-off we would climb out of the clouds and break into intense sunshine, with the clouds no longer gray but forming a pure white carpet below us. Soon the clouds would dissipate, and we almost always landed in clear, blindingly bright sunshine in Minnesota. How encouraging it was, in that long chronic illness of my Dad and my sorrow in preparing to lose him, to know that there were blue skies and sun above all my rain! To know that God had a purpose and a plan, and that He would never let me go!

If you are going through a dark, gray season of life with no apparent end in sight, try drawing near to God. He will draw near to you. Seek His purpose and rely on His love. Let Him comfort you in your despair. He is no cake-eater. He understands and He cares!

The Lord is like a father to his children, tender and compassionate to those who fear him. For he knows how weak we are; he remembers we are only dust.

Psalm 103:13-14

He Understands

If I had to wake up and face this alone
If I had to carry this cross on my own and face the day ahead –
I couldn't get out of bed!
If I had to explain what has happened to me
If I tried to describe this reality – Oh, it would break my heart
I wouldn't know where to start!

But I know that there is blue sky and sun above all this rain
And I know that God can somehow turn loss to gain!

And he understands when a grief can't be spoken
He understands disappointment and pain
He understands what it means to be broken, and to rise again
He made the world, and he knows that I'm in it,
He's not a distant observer or an eye in the sky
He's right by my side, every hour, every minute
And he knows why –
He understands!

At times when my heart is covered with fear
He says, "Rest in my arms, and I will be here to comfort you."
And that's what I'm going to do!
For eyes have not seen, and ears have not heard
No mind can conceive what God has prepared for those who love him
And I love him!

And I know that my Redeemer lives, and I'll see his face
And when I can't go on that's when he gives more grace

And he understands when a grief can't be spoken
He understands disappointment and pain
He understands what it means to be broken, and to rise again

He made the world, and he knows that I'm in it,
He's not a distant observer or an eye in the sky
He's right by my side, every hour, every minute
And he knows why –
He understands!

CHAPTER 6

It Was Never Meant to End This Way

My Mom developed Parkinson's disease in her early 80's, and it was a very difficult journey. Optimistic and sunny by nature, but also prone to anxiety, it was sad to see her gradually lose her independence. As she became weaker and more rigid in her movement, she began to fall frequently. Ultimately, she progressed to assisted-living and finally to total nursing care. Throughout the years of her illness, I frequently visited her on my way home from work, often at dinnertime to help feed her. Eating became very hard, since she had poor appetite, and her swallowing was weak. In the end she was completely bedridden, unable to even shift her position in bed. Talking was difficult because her mouth was so dry, and at times in the days before she died, I would just sit on the edge of her bed and stare at her beautiful face as she slept. I was overwhelmed by the brutality of her suffering and disease, by her emaciated body, and by the memory of her joyful vitality and faith that had infused my life with so much joy.

As a physician, every fiber in my being wanted to fix the situation, and I was always pushing to regain lost ground. I encouraged her to take one more bite, one more step, one more wheelchair ride outside to the garden. I wanted to change the course of her relentless disease and alleviate her suffering, but in truth I was powerless.

I visited her the night before she died. It was difficult to arouse her, but she finally awakened and consented to get up in her wheelchair. I took her to the dining room and lifted the spoon to her lips, but she could only manage a few bites and a few sips. I took her out into the courtyard to feel the warm sun on her face and hear her beloved birds, but she was distant. As I sat beside her, she just looked at me, unable to talk in an audible voice. Her eyes seemed to reflect frustration, a resignation, and a yearning. As I gazed into her eyes, I thought in my heart, "It was never meant to end this way. God didn't create us for death and suffering." Early the next morning, Mom passed into the glorious presence of her Savior.

I understand the challenge that human suffering and death present to those who are skeptical of faith. Many could sum up their skepticism in this way:

> *A god, for me to call it god and worship it as such, would have to be loving at all times; eliminating evil, violence, suffering, and aging for everyone, including me. It could never allow atrocities and natural disasters. In other words, the only god I would ever believe in is the one who provides a perfect world - heaven on earth!*

That's a reasonable expectation of God, and that's what He did! The Bible states that God created a perfect world, but we brought sin and death into that world when we aspired to be His equal, when we refused to worship Him as God, when we wanted to set ourselves up as our own authority. We all have sinned against the Holy God, and there is no one who is 100% righteous in their own effort. Now we suffer the consequences of our deadly rebellion - the suffering and evil that our own hearts have produced. But God, in His faithful love, did not leave us without remedy. Read the description of Jesus' rescue mission from Isaiah 53:1-6:

> Who has believed our message?
> > To whom has the Lord revealed his powerful arm?
> My servant grew up in the Lord's presence like a tender green shoot,
> > like a root in dry ground.
> There was nothing beautiful or majestic about his appearance,
> > nothing to attract us to him.
> He was despised and rejected—
> > a man of sorrows, acquainted with deepest grief.
> We turned our backs on him and looked the other way.
> > He was despised, and we did not care.
> Yet it was our weaknesses he carried;
> > it was our sorrows that weighed him down.
> And we thought his troubles were a punishment from God,
> > a punishment for his own sins!
> But he was pierced for our rebellion,
> > crushed for our sins.
> He was beaten so we could be whole.
> > He was whipped so we could be healed.
> All of us, like sheep, have strayed away.
> > We have left God's paths to follow our own.
> Yet the Lord laid on him
> > the sins of us all.

Jesus is God's response - His solution - to the self-inflicted pain and suffering of those He created and loves. It is His unbelievable love that led Him to voluntarily join us in our pain, and He provided a way of escape - a permanent, eternal solution - which gives hope and courage during trials. He gives the promise of eternal life, but beyond that, He comforts us and ministers to us in our present struggle. The old hymn says it best,

> "Help for today, and bright hope for tomorrow
> Blessings all mine, with ten thousand beside!"

What more can God do! Far from negating the existence of God, sickness and death point us to the overwhelming love and grace of God. The hopelessness and meaninglessness of life, so exposed in illness and death, is conquered and reversed by our redeeming, loving God! What soul, liberated from sin and its eternal, dreadful consequences, would not cry out to His glory?

> "Oh, for a thousand tongues to sing my great redeemer's praise!"

As It Was Meant to Be

It was never meant to end this way
It was not His plan on creation day
When He stretched out a loving hand
To create a woman and a man
The parents of our human race
Could talk to God and see His face
They walked with Him in harmony
In a perfect world
As it was meant to be

Unique in our humanity
The image of His deity
We were free to think and feel and choose
Free to win, and free to lose
But perfection turned to tragedy
When we rejected God's authority
Our souls received a mortal wound
And death was born
It was never meant to be

And now with bodies' failing certainty
We are flailing for eternity
We long for everlasting life
To be innocent of sin and strife
And God, who sees our great despair
Became a man, and met us there
He bore our pain and misery
To set us free
As it was meant to be

Amazing love! How can it be?
That God Most High would die -
That God would die -
That God would die for me!

So tell me now what you would do
If you were God, and He was you
What price would you agree to give
So your lost and wayward child could live?
Come rest now, weak and weary one
In the loving arms of God's own Son
Come know His mercy, grace, and peace
Forevermore,
As it was meant to be

All of us, like sheep, have strayed away. We have left God's paths to follow our own. Yet the Lord laid on him the sins of us all.

Isaiah 53:6

CHAPTER 7

Angola

You never know what the day holds when you are a surgeon, and how it might change your life. Several years ago, I was called to the hospital by one of my partners to do an emergency heart surgery on a patient. What was unusual about the situation was that by the time I arrived, the patient was already down in the OR, so I did not have an opportunity to meet him before the case began. Fortunately, everything went well, and when I came out to talk to his wife, she told me she had been praying for me, which I appreciated. Then she added, "And Billy Graham has been praying for you, too." What? Why was the famous evangelist Billy Graham praying for me?

It turns out that my patient had worked for Billy Graham for thirty years, managing the logistics for several of his huge evangelistic meetings. Even in his retirement, he was still assisting Billy Graham's daughter Ruth Graham, who had a unique ministry reaching out to people who are often forgotten in the church or in our society. My patient is a dynamo, and he said, "Doc, why don't you come with us on our next trip?

Angola

We're going down to Louisiana to a famous prison farm known as Angola. There are literally hundreds of prisoners who have become Christians there and we will go down to encourage them."

Perhaps you have heard of Angola. For decades it was the most infamous prison in America, a hopeless and violent place with a history of unspeakable brutality, buried in a pocket of the deep South along a bend in the Mississippi River where the battles of the Civil War never reached. It is a place where the majority of the 6200 inmates will eventually die in prison. I ended up going on that trip – in fact I went twice. And what I experienced there changed my life forever. I met murderers and rapists and kidnappers and every other sort of criminal, who were finding forgiveness and love in the words of Jesus, finding compassion for their victims and families, taking responsibility, and then putting God's love in action. I saw them serving their fellow inmates after long days working in the fields. I saw them tenderly caring for the sick and dying in their prison hospice unit. I saw them preaching the Word of God, worshiping in song, memorizing Scripture. I saw them reaching out to their own sons and daughters and parenting from prison, trying to end the cycle of violence and incarceration in their families. It was nothing short of miraculous.

When I sat down on the plane in Baton Rouge to return after my first trip, I buckled my seat belt, and as the plane pushed back I started to cry. I couldn't help it - it was embarrassing! The tears kept coming until we landed in Memphis for my connecting flight. The poor young man who sat next to me was really uncomfortable! But I was simply overwhelmed by so much I had seen and heard. I've known some suffering in my own life, but when you enter a high security prison you see suffering focused like a laser beam. The guilt, the regret, the violence, the missed opportunities, the wasted talents. Most of these inmates have destroyed two families – the victim's and their own. Many of them end up forgotten by their families after a few years. Life goes on without them, and they are left to hopeless despair. But what I saw in those Christian inmates was not despair. It was intense, but it was not despair. There was regret, but not despair. There was grim reality all around them, but not despair. There was incredible hope, incredible joy, incredible peace. They had found forgiveness in Jesus. They recognized that Jesus bore their brokenness on the cross.

We are living in the days of cancel culture, which means that anything you have ever said or done can and will be used against you! We are a society that cannot forgive each other. But forgiveness is essential, especially in suffering. We all need it, and we need to give it to others. When we are suffering, we feel burdened by our own sins, but we also feel the burden of those who have sinned against us. In Christ we find an answer – He forgives our sin so that we can forgive ourselves, and then we can seek forgiveness from others, and we can offer forgiveness to others who have abused us. Isn't that what's needed in our society today? Don't we see the devastating effects of the cycle of bitterness in our world? Jesus touched on this with his parable about a man who was forgiven a huge debt, only to selfishly refuse to forgive a much smaller debt that he was owed.

Billy Graham's family has a long history of association with the prison at Angola. He and his wife are both buried in simple oak caskets lovingly built by inmates there. He traveled the world and spoke to millions in some of the largest stadium venues of his day, but his heart was touched by the powerful stories of forgiveness and redemption he found in that prison, and he loved the inmates there. His family donated money to help build a beautiful church, with a steeple visible for miles within the farm. Atop that steeple is a cross – a powerful symbol in its design. Every cross depicts God's outstretched arms of love in the horizontal, and His forgiveness pouring down in the vertical. God's arms are open wide with forgiveness! Come to Him in your brokenness and know that He cares for every detail in your life. He will be there for you to help and strengthen you by His presence as you face profound fear, and He will forgive your sins when you confess them to God in repentance. I John 1:9 offers this wonderful promise:

> But if we confess our sins to him, he is faithful and just to forgive us our sins and to cleanse us from all wickedness.

If you are facing a time of suffering, and it is compounded by a sense of guilt before God or bitterness for wrongs you have suffered, please consider reaching out to God for forgiveness. It is a prayer He is bound to answer by His promise. He wants to set you free and heal you deep in your soul - if you will let Him in!

If we confess our sins to him, he is faithful and just to forgive us our sins and to cleanse us from all wickedness.

1 John 1:9

Forgiveness

It's a voice that haunts you in the dark of night
You've done wrong and you can't make it right
It's a lonely song and you think you might need forgiveness
Don't let your guilt make you run away
Don't waste time searching for some words to say
Just run to Jesus and he'll lead the way
To forgiveness

Oh, forgiveness, forgiveness
We all need forgiveness
And it's the centerpiece of faith
The evidence of grace
Reflection of the face of God –
We need forgiveness!

Now we all fall short, and we all have sinned
We all have wandered far away from him
But he freely offers perfect peace within through forgiveness
And when you find that peace, you'll know what to do
You forgive all men as God's forgiven you
And with a heart that's cleansed you can start anew
With forgiveness

Oh, forgiveness, forgiveness
We all need forgiveness
And it's the centerpiece of faith
The evidence of grace
Reflection of the face of God –
We need forgiveness!

If we won't forgive, we're like the man with a million-dollar debt
He couldn't pay, so he faced a life of misery, and yet
When his loving master pitied him and set him free he still
Put another man in prison for a hundred-dollar bill!
Or we're like the group of lepers Jesus healed along the way
You think they'd be so grateful, but only one returned to say it
And if you know it was the King of Kings that hung there on that cross
Imagine what he suffered to recover what we lost!

And that's forgiveness, forgiveness
We all need forgiveness
And it's the centerpiece of faith
The evidence of grace
Reflection of the face of God –
We need forgiveness!

Have you seen the cross where Jesus died?
His love flowing down and reaching side to side
It's an invitation, his arms open wide
With forgiveness
Forgiveness!

CHAPTER 8

Grace

One of the character traits I love best about God is His knowability – God has made Himself known to us through His Word, the Bible. He allows us to see Him as He really is and welcomes us into a relationship with Him. That's not something we should take for granted. How many great athletes, or celebrities, or world leaders, have made themselves known to you? We may be able to follow them on Instagram, but imagine walking up to their front door and saying, "Hey, I just really want to know you better. Let's hang out and talk, and share some secrets, and watch a movie!" That would be a great way to meet someone from their security detail, but not the celebrities themselves. They have intentionally decided not to make themselves known. But God has invited us to know Him intimately, and the burden is on us if we fail to seek Him in truth and instead embrace a false notion of Him. God wants to comfort us in our suffering, but a false notion of God cannot bring comfort.

Many people embrace the false notion that God bases His rewards on a merit system - He promises benefits, but only if you meet certain requirements. You must love Him enough, you must follow Him enough, you must please Him enough, you must impress Him enough. If you do, then you might get some great benefits. This false notion takes on a few different forms. I've had patients who refuse to discuss or even acknowledge the severity of their illness because they are convinced that they will only be cured if they demonstrate total faith. Theirs is a language of denial. Others don't feel deserving of God's benefits. They don't feel deserving of God's deliverance. Theirs is the language of defeat. Even though they may know that God can do great and wonderful things, they don't really believe that He'll do it for them. They think, "He may be a great, loving, powerful and forgiving God, but probably not in my case. And that's because I know I have some deficiency in my life, or some dark sin in my past. I just don't think God wants me to be happy, and I don't think I deserve it."

Years ago, I took care of a patient who was a single man in his mid 50's. He lived alone and said he had very little contact with any family or friends. As we became acquainted, he described a very sad and reclusive life. Unfortunately, he had developed a life-threatening disease in his lungs, and he was referred to me for a surgical lung biopsy. Prior to his surgery he confided in me that he was terrified to die, and I asked him about his faith story. He stated that he was from a religious background but not really going to church. I offered to pray for him, and he accepted that very gladly. After the surgery his lungs deteriorated further, and he was dependent on the ventilator – we couldn't wean him off. As days went by without improvement, our care team became more concerned that we were only prolonging his suffering. I kept praying he would improve enough to come off the ventilator and his sedation, so he would have a chance to resolve his spiritual confusion and fear. He had expressed his remorse and guilt to me. He was afraid of where he would go upon death, and I prayed he would have another chance to come to peace with God.

Miraculously, my patient did improve, and the breathing tube was taken out. When he was able to talk, I knew that I needed to go into his room and at least offer to talk about faith with him. I had requested a chaplain, thinking that a professional would be better, but none was available. It seemed God had called me in that moment, and so I asked the nurse to leave us alone for about an hour. I went into his ICU room and closed the door, not knowing what to say. It turned out I didn't need to know because the patient started. He said, "Do you know what I heard in these last two weeks while I was on the ventilator? It sounded like the ventilator was saying, "Cut, cut, kill, kill, die, die." He went on to express remorse for bad things he had done. He did not feel worthy of forgiveness or help from God. In moments like these, when we are transparent and vulnerable, we can hear the words of Scripture with a fresh clarity. The verse we read together was Ephesians 2:8-9:

> God saved you by his grace when you believed. And you can't take credit for this; it is a gift from God. Salvation is not a reward for the good things we have done, so none of us can boast about it.

It was like a breath of fresh air filling his lungs when he heard that verse. He had never learned of God's grace. He had always been taught that we earn our salvation by doing good works, and he was certain his moral balance sheet was in the red. But this verse was an incredible revelation to Him. God's gift of salvation

Grace

is made possible by the grace of God.

2 Timothy 1:9-10 states it well:

> For God saved us and called us to live a holy life. He did this, not because we deserved it, but because that was his plan from before the beginning of time—to show us his grace through Christ Jesus. And now he has made all of this plain to us by the appearing of Christ Jesus, our Savior. He broke the power of death and illuminated the way to life and immortality through the Good News.

As my patient and I considered the marvelous grace and love of God, he became more hopeful. He invited me to pray again, and then it was a joy to hear him invite Jesus into that moment, asking for a sense of His presence and forgiveness, offering a humble and sincere prayer of faith. In the days that followed he also spoke with our chaplain. Lacking the strength to read, he lay in his bed with earphones on, listening to the book of John and then the Psalms. His physical improvements were only temporary, and he became more oxygen dependent, but his spiritual peace was eternal. God had used his season of suffering to bring about an amazing transformation in his life. He died peacefully 2 weeks later.

Suffering interrupts our routine and injects uncertainty into our life. In any typical day, we find much of our sense of value and identity in our relationships, our possessions, our job, and activities. When everything comes to a screeching halt – we lose a spouse, we lose a child, we are in pain, we are facing a severe illness – there is a real loss of value. This leads to a sense of worthlessness – we feel unworthy and undeserving of God's love.

We think, "You know, I haven't really followed God perfectly all my life, why should I expect to receive anything from Him now?" But that's what makes it grace! If God only gives you what you deserve, there's no mercy or grace in that! God's unbelievable grace is unmerited – it's nothing we control or can take credit for. Remember these encouraging words from Psalms 103: 10-12?

> He does not punish us for all our sins:
> he does not deal harshly with us, as we deserve.
> For his unfailing love toward those who fear him
> is as great as the height of the heavens above the earth.
> He has removed our sins as far from us
> as the east is from the west.

In an earlier chapter I described my experience at Angola prison. Can you imagine how hard it is for a convicted murderer in prison at Angola to see himself as worthy to receive the free gift of eternal life from God? What about us? We are so conditioned in our different religious traditions to think that God only awards the most pious, the most perfect among us. We hope we have done enough to deserve God's favor, but in the end, we are worried that we haven't. There is no peace or comfort in that. But three words describe God's unexpected response – Grace, Mercy, Love. Grace speaks to receiving something we don't deserve. Mercy speaks to not being punished in a way we do deserve. And God's love is strong and unconditional – not based on performance or perfection. God loves you, right now, just the way you are – mistakes, failures, and all – and He always has loved you like that. The forgiveness and eternal life He gives is based on His holiness, not ours. Unattainable by human effort, it is not under our control. It is not something God gives based on merit. If it was, it wouldn't be grace, mercy, or true love. When we draw near to Him in our weakness and humility of heart, He draws near to us with forgiveness and love. Remember, Jesus walked among us as a man. He knows what we are facing, and He is full of compassion!

That's What Makes It Grace

Nothing grieves me more
Than seeing you come face to face with Jesus
And then closing your heart's door,
Because you think that you're not good enough to please him
You say, "Even if it's true, I wouldn't deserve it."
Well, it is true, and you're right, you don't deserve it
And neither do I

That's what makes it grace
That's what makes it love
That's what makes it mercy, unconditional and strong
Nothing you earn or take control of
Only Someone pure can take the stain away
And make the scales fall from our eyes
So we can see His face
That's what makes it grace

You don't know what I've done, and I can't see where you've been
We both have battles lost and won,
And I don't know if I'm better than other men
But I do know on the cross, He loved me first
And even though he saw me at my worst
He still paid it all

That's what makes it grace
That's what makes it love
That's what makes it mercy, unconditional and strong
Nothing you earn or take control of
Only Someone pure can take the stain away
And make the scales fall from our eyes
So we can see His face
That's what makes it grace

Unlimited forgiveness, free and unrestricted
Jesus came and lifted the burden of
My soul - will live forever, my weaknesses can never
Separate me from the great redeeming love of God!

That's what makes it grace
That's what makes it love
That's what makes it mercy, unconditional and strong
Nothing you earn or take control of
Only Someone pure can take the stain away
And make the scales fall from our eyes
So we can see His face
And know the miracle of grace!

He'll open up your eyes so you can see His face
And His marvelous grace.
That's what makes it grace!

For his unfailing love toward those who fear him is as great as the height of the heavens above the earth.

Psalm 103:11

CHAPTER 9

Invitation

Everybody has a faith story. Everybody has a life journey that includes some level of relationship with God. When I was a kid growing up in a very evangelical church, we had frequent altar-calls, or "invitations." As a child, I was always ready to go forward, because my heart was easily pierced by the message of the Gospel, and I felt compelled to respond as an act of obedience to God's leading. As I became older, I became more proud, more self-conscious. I would feel the same tug on my heart, but I could more easily invent reasons not to walk down the aisle. I reasoned that if I responded too much it would dilute the meaning of my response, or make it seem insincere. In time I became almost impervious to the call, with a fully rationalized adult resistance to almost any public display of humility or need. As I look back now, however, I realize that those unquestioning public displays of devotion and commitment were an important part of my faith story. They were high points of faith that marked my road to a deeper relationship with God.

Perhaps you also sat through altar-calls as a child and heard the invitations. They're not very common now in most churches, which in a way is a shame. Our world has never seemed more fragmented or barren than it does now. Our souls are so easily deadened by the noise that surrounds us that we have lost any attentiveness to God and His voice. That's why Jesus said, "He who has ears to hear, let them hear." If God is tugging at your heart right now, if you are welling with emotion in the midst of your suffering and pain and you long for the touch of God, then let your spiritual ears hear! If God issues another familiar invitation to come to Him, don't resist Him! He is using your trial to draw you to Him.

God's love for you is powerful and strong. He's not exhausted, He's never terrified or surprised. And He will never give up on you, because He has had you in mind for a long, long time! His commitment to you is deep and personal, to the extent that He desires to adopt you into His own family. Ephesians 1:4-8 says,

> Even before he made the world, God loved us and chose us in Christ to be holy and without fault in his eyes. God decided in advance to adopt us into his own family by bringing us to himself through Jesus Christ. This is what he wanted to do, and it gave him great pleasure. So we praise God for the glorious grace he has poured out on us who belong to his dear Son. He is so rich in kindness and grace that he purchased our freedom with the blood of his Son and forgave our sins. He has showered his kindness on us, along with all wisdom and understanding.

God is so rich in kindness and grace that He purchased our freedom at the expense of His own Son. Freedom from eternal death, freedom from the power of sin, freedom to be all we were meant to be! Our sufferings make us attentive and

Invitation

help us open our ears to hear His voice. They beckon us to take the next step in our faith journey as we respond to His invitation!

> Then Jesus said, "Come to me, all of you who are weary and carry heavy burdens, and I will give you rest."
> — Matthew 11:28

Then Jesus said, "Come to me, all of you who are weary and carry heavy burdens, and I will give you rest."

Matthew 11:28

Come to Jesus

It's a familiar invitation, it's been repeated through the years
So many times you've heard it, but it's fallen on deaf ears
But tonight it seems so simple, somehow personal and real
It's as if the God who's calling knows exactly how you feel.

Come to Jesus, let him turn your life around
Walk away from all the fear and guilt
That have thrown you to the ground
And let him love you, let him heal your broken heart
Let the power of forgiveness give your life a brand-new start
And come to Jesus.

You say your life is full of conflict, and you're yearning for some peace
You're struggling with addiction and you just cannot find release
And they said they'd never leave you until the day they walked away
And now your life's so dark and lonely, it's hard to face another day

Come to Jesus, let him turn your life around
Walk away from all the fear and guilt
That have thrown you to the ground
And let him love you, let him heal your broken heart
Let the power of forgiveness give your life a brand-new start
And come to Jesus.

CHAPTER 10

A Healing Stream Will Flow

I will never forget my first day of medical school. It was the culmination of many years of diligent study and planning. Since childhood I had felt the calling to be a physician, and on Day One I was overwhelmed with emotion. I looked around the room at my fellow students, and I wondered if I could compete. My mind was spinning with the details of the orientation. And then there was the moment when I knew I was crossing a line into a world that very few people were allowed to cross. That was the moment I "met" my cadaver in anatomy lab. It was odd enough finding my way to the musty hall upstairs in the antiquated building that housed the anatomy lab, changing into throw-away clothes in the hallway in front of small metal lockers, surrounded in full view of other classmates – strangers still – who were also changing clothes and donning their white lab coats. Then I entered the pathology lab with its strange odor and stared with a mixture of wonder and dread at the cadaver laying on a table before me. I remember thinking, "In any other context, this would be so wrong. Society has given me a pass into a different zone of human interaction – one which allows me to dissect dead people, one that allows me to touch the bodies of people I do not know, one that allows me to inflict injury on others – all for the sake of relieving suffering and healing disease." As I drove home that first day my mind was racing. I was so distracted that I ran right through a red light in a busy intersection and was T-boned by another car. No injuries to anyone, but my car was undriveable, and in that pre-cell phone era I remember calling my Dad from a pay phone in the corner bar. That memory, however, is quite minor and vague. The first day of medical school was just that overwhelming.

In total I went through 17 and a half years of post-high school education before I took my first job in practice. Through it all I was equipping myself for a sacred responsibility - to alleviate human suffering. I came to realize that most people do not voluntarily involve themselves in the suffering of others. They have empathy and concern, but they do not want to be the actual one making the incision, prescribing the medications, or delivering the bad news. Some are squeamish at the sight of blood. Some are overwhelmed with the fear that illness and medical facilities invoke. For me, I never wanted to be anywhere else. Ministering to those who are suffering felt like the most Christian thing I could do. Not just caring for my own but caring for those who were not my own. I know this is not just limited to Christians, or to those in the medical profession, but for me this was the center of my calling and vocation.

After medical school, which was intense and competitive, I entered the world of general surgical residency, which brought a whole different level of intensity. Long, sleepless nights and long stressful days were the norm. My surgical mentors were decent, kind teachers. They were at times critical and demanding, as they needed to be, since they were preparing me to function independently in decision-making and in the operating room. Surgical residency was relentlessly intense, sometimes traumatic, often exciting, and always exhausting. During that time, I developed some dear friendships with a few other residents and their families. We supported and cared for each other in the battle and emerged with a depth of understanding that can only be achieved by sharing intense, life-changing experiences. We were like veterans with our war stories of residency, which were a mixture of sometimes painful and occasionally hilarious moments. These were friends who saw me at my best and my worst and loved me anyway.

Steve and Kim were two of those precious friends. Steve and I went through surgical residency together, and Kim and my wife Sara were young wives trying to get by with no money and a husband that was never home. Residents routinely worked 100-hour weeks back then, so our friendships were forged in fire, and after residency we stayed in touch as best as we could as we went out to establish our practices and raise our kids. Sara and I ultimately came back to the Twin Cities, and Steve and Kim settled in Iowa. Kim had lost several close relatives to breast cancer, and then we were sad to learn she had developed it as well. It was an aggressive tumor that ultimately spread throughout her system, leading her through a 13-year battle, with Steve and their beautiful children lovingly by her side.

I wish everyone could have known Kim. She had a sweetness, a delicate grace, and a selfless love for all around her. Her voice was the sound of kindness itself. She radiated the love and joy of Jesus even as her strength was failing. She demonstrated the supernatural peace and power of God. Finally, we received a call that her journey was nearing the end, and we prepared to drive down to Iowa to see her one last time. My wife made a meal for the family, and while she was working on that, I was suddenly prompted to write a song, which I shared with Kim that same day. As she lay in her bed at home surrounded by her family, I sat at the piano in the living room and sang through tears. The message of the song is simple, and it was what God gave me in that sacred moment. It is the assurance that in the middle of our darkest trial, God is there.

An incredible story was told at Kim's funeral, of a different woman battling breast cancer who was facing her first day of chemotherapy. She was frightened, grieving, dreading the experience. As she sat in the waiting room, another patient reached out to her, offering her calm words of comfort and advice. That patient expressed understanding and compassion for her, answering her questions and reassuring her that God was with her, and she would do well. Later the woman recounted her experience to her surgeon. She felt as though she had been visited by an angel, so comforting and peaceful was her presence, so empowering were her words. As she described the encounter, her surgeon was flooded with emotion. The surgeon was my friend Steve, and the angel in the waiting room was Kim! She was the very presence of God for that woman who was overcome by fear on that disorienting and overwhelming day.

There is a loneliness in suffering - the feeling of the lost lamb left behind, stumbling alone through the storm as the flock moves safely on without you. But with Jesus you are never lost. A hundred people can walk by you in a day and never know the heartache and fear you feel in your soul, but Jesus sees you and comes looking for you. He knows and He cares. Listen to the parable He told from Luke 15:3-7:

> So Jesus told them this story: "If a man has a hundred sheep and one of them gets lost, what will he do? Won't he leave the ninety-nine others in the wilderness and go to search for the one that is lost until he finds it? And when he has found it, he will joyfully carry it home on his shoulders. When he arrives, he will call together his friends and neighbors, saying, 'Rejoice with me because I have found my lost sheep.' In the same way, there is more joy in heaven over one lost sinner who repents and returns to God than over ninety-nine others who are righteous and haven't strayed away!

Jesus said, "I am the good shepherd. The good shepherd sacrifices his life for the sheep." Jesus literally laid down His life for you and for me. If you are lost in a wilderness of confusion and pain, cry out to Jesus, the same way a lamb cries out in distress. Jesus will come beside you, with gentleness and healing, and He will see you through. What we seek is ultimate healing – hope for eternity in the presence of a loving God, free from sickness, pain, uncertainty. That was the hope that sustained us in our sad last visit with Kim, which I will never forget. Tears? Yes. Disappointment and sadness? Yes - definitely. But through it all a deep sense of God's presence and the assurance that we will see each other again. And that made all the difference. God saw Kim through – 13 years as a Mom living with cancer, losing her strength, entrusting her family to God, and finally walking through the dark valley into the glorious light of Jesus! God loves you just as deeply, and He will see you through!

Don't be afraid, for I am with you.
Don't be discouraged, for I am your God.
I will strengthen you and help you.
I will hold you up with my victorious right hand.
— Isaiah 41:10

Kim's Song

I know you hurt, and the days are long
I won't pretend that by singing a song
I can ease your pain or make you strong
I'm not the place where your hope belongs.

When the mountains shake, and the fire rains,
And it feels like you're taking a hurricane
If you stop and listen, you'll hear his voice
Calling out in the confusion and the noise

And then a gentle wind will blow
A healing stream will flow
And speak comfort to your soul
That God is in control
Be still and know that He is God!
And he loves you
And he will save you
He will see you through

It's an unknown path, but you're never lost
Because he will find you at any cost
Because he's the shepherd and you're his lamb
Come and rest in his tender hand

And then a gentle wind will blow
A healing stream will flow
And speak comfort to your soul
That God is in control
Be still and know that He is God!
And he loves you
And he will save you
He will see you through!

Don't be afraid, for I am with you. Don't be discouraged, for I am your God. I will strengthen you and help you. I will hold you up with my victorious right hand.

Isaiah 41:10

CHAPTER 11

Receiving the Gift of Life

I went to medical school at the University of Minnesota, and I am proud of my alma mater. With open heart surgery performed routinely in community hospitals around the world, it is often taken for granted that dramatic repairs can be safely performed on human hearts. But this was not always the case. In fact, dating back to the early 1950's, surgeons lacked the technology to safely support a patient's circulation in a way that would allow intra-cardiac defects to be repaired. Children born with various congenital heart defects routinely died at a young age from heart failure. How could the heart be opened and repaired without temporarily stopping it, and how could a patient be kept alive during that time? Several centers worked simultaneously in the mid 1950's in a friendly but intense competition, a race to develop an artificial blood oxygenator and pump system that could function in place of a patients' heart and lungs while their heart was being repaired. The epicenter of this research was in Minnesota, both at the University of Minnesota and 90 miles down the road at the Mayo Clinic. The proposed "heart-lung" machines were full of potential dangers. How could blood be interfaced with oxygen in such a way that the blood cells were not destroyed? What was the ideal tubing and pump system, and what was the proper rate of flow? How could patients' blood be thinned to prevent clotting throughout the system and their bodies, and how could the bleeding then be stopped when the procedure was finished?

Various research teams attacked these problems with furious passion, aided by technology giants such as IBM and General Motors. But there was one pioneer that stood out above the rest – C. Walton Lillehei at the University of Minnesota. A surgeon of stunning skill, courage bordering on recklessness, and an inquisitive mind that could think outside the box, he grew impatient with the mechanical and looked to the biological for a solution. Realizing that every pregnant mother serves as an oxygenator for her fetus via the placenta, he developed a technique for open heart surgery utilizing "cross-circulation." In this daring procedure, one of a child's parents served as the heart and lung for their child while the child's heart was opened and repaired. Cannulas, or plastic tubes, were connected between the parent's vascular system and the child's heart, allowing red oxygenated blood to pass from the parent to the child, and blue blood to return from the child to the parent's vein, which would then feed it to the parent's lungs for oxygen. The arrangement allowed the surgical team to briefly stop and open the child's heart and make the necessary repair. In those brief moments, the child's life was in the parent's blood! Using cross-circulation, Dr Lillehei performed 45 open heart operations over the course of 15 months, and the world stood in awe of his accomplishments. The cross-circulation technique was never widely adopted, largely because it carried a potential 200% mortality rate if both the child and the parent were to die from complications, but it ushered in the modern era of heart surgery, and Dr Lillehei is widely regarded as the "Father of Open Heart Surgery."

I imagine that, although frightening, it was an easy decision for the parents who chose to save their child in those cross-circulation surgeries. Many times during the course of my surgical career, I have heard grieving parents say, "I wish I could trade places with my child and take the suffering on myself." It is in the nature of any loving parent to stand between suffering and their child, and to prevent pain at any cost, even cost to themselves. Is it so hard to understand, then, that our loving God was willing to lay down His life for us? The Old Testament system of animal sacrifice was based on the shedding of innocent blood for the forgiveness of sins. It was a foreshadowing of the ultimate blood sacrifice that God Himself would pay to redeem His people once and for all from the deadly consequences of their rebellion. When Jesus' blood was shed on the cross, it was poured out for us as the perfect sacrifice for our sins. This is why at the Last Supper, Jesus said, "This cup is the new covenant in my blood, which is poured out for you." We are redeemed by the blood of Jesus, as described in I Peter 1:18-19:

> For you know that God paid a ransom to save you from the empty life you inherited from your ancestors. And it was not paid with mere gold or silver, which lose their value. It was the precious blood of Christ, the sinless, spotless Lamb of God.

There is life in the blood of Jesus!

For so many, a deeper relationship with God begins with some fundamental realizations that are summed up by the Apostle

Paul in several famous verses from the Book of Romans:

1. **We are all sinners and have fallen short of God's perfection.**

    "for all have sinned and fall short of the glory of God."
    — Romans 3:23

2. **Our sin separates us from God and results in death.**

    "for the wages of sin is death." — Romans 6:23a

3. **God in His love provided a way for our redemption.**

    "But God demonstrates his own love for us in this: While we were still sinners, Christ died for us." — Romans 5:8

4. **God offers life through His Son Jesus as a gift, which is stunning in that we do not have to worry about earning it through our own merits.**

    "the gift of God is eternal life in Christ Jesus our Lord."
    — Romans 6:23b

5. **We receive the gift of salvation through faith.**

    "and all are justified freely by his grace through the redemption that came by Christ Jesus. God presented Christ as a sacrifice of atonement, through the shedding of his blood—to be received by faith." — Romans 3:24-25

Once a person realizes that his or her life has been saved by a sacrificial gift that they neither earned or deserved, a gift offered purely out of love and at great personal cost to the giver, that person is forever grateful. Many of Dr Lillehei's young patients lived into full adulthood. Imagine the intimate bond they shared with their parents who had willingly risked their own lives on their behalf! Jesus said, "There is no greater love than to lay down one's life for one's friends." This is why the Christian life is not one of rules and regulations, or endless "religious" requirements, but one of worship, gratitude, and joy. When Christians speak of a "personal relationship with God," they are not attempting to bring God down to their level or cheapen the value of His mercy and grace. They are simply acknowledging that God Himself reached out in love and saved them, personally, through His death on the cross and resurrection from the grave. They share an intimate connection with their Savior – their life is in His blood! Inspired by His sacrifice and perfection, they seek to follow Him in a life of service and to share the Good News with others.

Any personal relationship begins with communication and grows with shared experiences, so let your relationship with God begin and then grow through prayer. Start by acknowledging your sin and your need for His gift. Tell God that you need His forgiveness and want to turn away from your sin. Thank Him for the sacrifice of Jesus, and the free gift of salvation through His blood. Then go beyond a mere acknowledgement and receive the gift as your own. Declare Him not as "the Lord," but "your Lord!" Let this be personal for you, because it was by His very deep personal love for you that you are saved! If you yearn for the love and comfort of God in your suffering, He is drawing you to His love and revealing Himself to you. Don't run away in your pain – run toward Him, right into His arms! You will never regret placing your faith in Him!

Jesus Take My Hand

Jesus take my hand, Jesus hear my prayer
I know I've sinned, wandered far from home
And I'm tired of running, tired of running
Savior of the world, you died and rose for me
Save me, use me,
I'm yours from this day on.

For the wages of sin is death, but the free gift of God is eternal life through Christ Jesus our Lord.

Romans 6:23

EPILOGUE

The Anchor

If you have ever spent time in Minneapolis, you will know it has a well-deserved name as the City of Lakes. In almost every neighborhood you will find a pond, a stream, or a lake, and so water is constantly in view. The largest lake in the area is Lake Minnetonka, a 14,000-acre collection of interconnected bays so beautiful that, after a brief visit, President William Howard Taft proposed to Congress that a summer White House be built here in 1911. That idea never panned out, but for the last 19 years my family has enjoyed boating on the lake. And although summertime offers water sports and endless recreation, I love boating in October, when the temperatures are cooler, the weather is blustery, the water is a deep cobalt blue, and thousands of sugar maples on the shore are in full colorful display. But since it is a time of year when few boaters remain, you do not want to experience a technical problem on the boat – the lonely, dreaded "dead in the water" experience!

That is exactly what happened to me several years ago. On a sunny fall day, I had invited several family and friends onto the boat to enjoy the fall colors. As is always the case, the wind was stronger and the air was colder than expected out on the lake, but my passengers were bundled-up and prepared. All was going well until the engine suddenly quit, and I could not get it restarted. We were now adrift with no power, far from our marina, and with very few boaters on the lake. The wind was strong and immediately started pushing the boat nearer to the shore, and I worried we would get hung up on rocks or beached in the sand. I was panicking! There was no combatting the force of the wind with the small oar I kept on board, no chance of waving down someone on the shore, where people were driving by blissfully unaware of our plight. Finally, as the water grew shallower, I jumped out of the boat and physically tried to walk it out to deeper water and keep it from drifting farther in. Finally, another boater came along and offered to tow us into a slip in a protected bay, where we could moor the boat and call for someone to pick us up. It was a rather nightmarish ending to a previously magical day!

It was not until later that evening, now warm and dry at home, with bruised pride at my failure as a boat captain, that I realized my critical oversight – a solution so obvious that it was laughable. All I needed to do in that moment we were adrift was to drop the anchor! Simply anchoring the boat would have protected my passengers, would have alleviated the stress of running aground, and it would have kept me out of the frigid water! We could have spent time trouble-shooting the mechanical problem, or calmly calling for help. But the whitecaps on the water, the looming rocks on the shore, and the disruption of our routine boat ride immediately set my mind reeling, and the anchor was never deployed.

The reason I share this story is that, in the last several weeks as

The Anchor

I have worked on the final layout for this book, my routine has been suddenly disrupted by a crisis that was totally unexpected. Over many years I had developed an increasingly painful and noticeable bump under my lower jaw. I had obtained several CT scans which appeared normal and were reassuring, but as the problem grew more obvious, I recently went in for another scan. This time the images were much more worrisome and led to a biopsy which revealed a salivary gland cancer, and this was followed days later by two surgeries to remove it. Surgery was successful and the margins are clear, but there were lymph nodes involved and the tumor had spread locally to involve nerves and muscles in my neck and mouth. A few nerves to my tongue and mouth had to be sacrificed, so this has changed the clarity of my speech and the appearance of my smile. I am recovering well, but I will begin radiation treatments soon. I am told that the long-term outlook is good due to the slow-growing nature of the cancer, but it could re-appear somewhere else, even decades down the line. The radiation may have side-effects that affect my voice. I have had to take a leave from work as I've entered the medical world not as physician, but now as a cancer patient!

In this sudden and unexpected change to my life, I could easily have been adrift in fear and despair, were it not for the anchor of my soul, Jesus Christ. This has been a sudden disruption to every routine in my life, like my "dead in the water" boating experience. The rest of the world carries on, unaware of the panic and pain in my heart and in our family. I am a person who does not like change. I like predictability. Like many physicians, I am a perfectionist, and I do not want to be the one needing help. As a songwriter, I like the words of my life to rhyme, and for everything to work together harmoniously, without the dissonance of looking different or sounding different. But I can honestly say that God

Epilogue

has met me moment-by-moment, and has surrounded me with His unfailing love, His goodness, His strength, and His forgiveness. God's forgiveness has been His most powerful gift to me, because the diagnosis of my cancer brought with it an overwhelming wave of regret and fear of God's rejection. It's hard to explain the evil spiritual accusations and attacks that we face in moments of crisis, but they are not from God. He wants us to draw close, He wants to forgive and forget, He wants to minister grace and comfort to our souls. He wants to show Himself real and strong on our behalf. He wants us to cry out to Him and turn to Him for help and healing. That is exactly what I have done, and He has not let me down. He has been my anchor.

My grandmother used to love the familiar phrase "God is good – all the time!" It wasn't because she had an easy life. It was because in her various trials she found that the character of God was immovable and His love was unfailing, no matter how turbulent her circumstances. In times of deep need, when our lives are painful and confusing and we feel isolated from God and those around us, we need an anchor for our souls. We need One who is bigger, stronger, more powerful than the waves that buffet our boat and are threatening to drive us into ruin. We need a God who is good all the time. Could this be the meaning behind one of the most famous events in Jesus' ministry, found in Mark 4:35-41?

> As evening came, Jesus said to his disciples, "Let's cross to the other side of the lake." So they took Jesus in the boat and started out, leaving the crowds behind (although other boats followed). But soon a fierce storm came up. High waves were breaking into the boat, and it began to fill with water. Jesus was sleeping at the back of the boat with his head on a cushion. The disciples woke him

up, shouting, "Teacher, don't you care that we're going to drown?" When Jesus woke up, he rebuked the wind and said to the waves, "Silence! Be still!" Suddenly the wind stopped, and there was a great calm. Then he asked them, "Why are you afraid? Do you still have no faith?" The disciples were absolutely terrified. "Who is this man?" they asked each other. "Even the wind and waves obey him!"

The winds and the waves obey Him! He is never overwhelmed. He is the anchor for our souls, firm and secure. His power and love are not affected by our circumstances. He has a plan for us, even when we feel that we might drown. He brings peace and great calm to our hurting hearts. I can confidently say from my present experience, without any doubt - He will meet you in your crisis and see you safely to the shore if you will turn your heart to Him. Cast all your anxiety on Him and cry out to Him, because He cares for you!

God is Good All the Time

When the road is long, and the chords don't fit the song I know
And everything sounds wrong to me –
Lord, I know you hear it too, and my road begins and ends in you
In you I find my harmony

God is good all the time, God is good all the time
When the words of life don't rhyme – God's still good!
God is good all the time, God is good all the time
When the words of life won't rhyme
God is good, God is good all the time!

"The Lord bless you real good!" my grandma used to say
It was her favorite way to say good-bye
I think she had a plan – she wanted us to see God's hand
In all the circumstances of our lives.

God is good all the time, God is good all the time
When the words of life don't rhyme – God's still good!
God is good all the time, God is good all the time
When the words of life won't rhyme
God is good, God is good all the time!

So run, run into His arms
The world with all its charms will never make you whole
And God knows your deepest fears, and He's promised to be near you
He's the anchor for your soul –
The anchor for your soul!

God is good all the time, God is good all the time
When the words of life don't rhyme – God's still good!
God is good all the time, God is good all the time
When the words of life won't rhyme
God is good, God is good all the time!

This hope is a strong and trustworthy anchor for our souls... Give all your worries and cares to God, for he cares about you.

Hebrews 6:19 & 1 Peter 5:7

About the Author

For the last 30 years, Mark Solfelt, MD has been ministering to people who are experiencing suffering. He is a cardiothoracic surgeon with an emphasis on lung surgery, and so he is actively involved in the treatment of those with various cancers and traumatic injuries involving the chest. He is also a musician and songwriter with a concert ministry called HealingStream. His music is designed to bring inspiration, hope, and healing to those who are suffering. Mark lives in the Midwest with his wife Sara. They are blessed with three wonderful children as well as two awesome son-in-laws. If you are able, please join Mark at a HealingStream concert – information is available at:

www.healingstreamevent.com